DATE DUE

JUN 2 6 2001	
OCT 2 0 2001	
FEB 2 3 2002	
APR 0 3 2004	
APR 1 5 2005	
NOV 2 6 2006	

LIVING WITH SNAKES

Eye to Eye with Snakes

Lynn M. Stone

Th[...] [...], Inc.
[...] 64

PHOTO CREDITS
© Marty Snyderman: p.6; © Joe McDonald: p.13,
18; © J.H. Pete Carmichael: cover, p. 22; © Lynn M. Stone:
title page, 4, 9, l0, 14, 15, 16, 21

EDITORIAL SERVICES
Penworthy Learning Systems

Library of Congress Cataloging-in-Publication Data

Stone, Lynn M.
    Living with snakes / Lynn M. Stone.
      p. cm. — (Eye to eye with snakes)
    Summary: Describes the different attitudes people have towards
snakes and discusses why they should be protected and their
habitats preserved.
    ISBN 1-55916-264-3
       1. Snakes—Juvenile literature. 2. Human-animal relationships —
Juvenile literature. [1.Snakes. 2. Human-animal relationships.] I.Title.

QL666.06 S8755 2000
597.96—dc21   00-025031

1-55916-264-3

Printed in the USA

CONTENTS

Fur buried in the loops of a rat snake marks the end of another rodent. Rat snakes are often called the farmers' "friends."

SNAKES AND PEOPLE

People often think of snakes as either friends or enemies. "Good" snakes kill mice and rats on the farm. They are our "friends." "Bad" snakes produce venom, or poison. These **venomous** snakes are our "enemies."

Snakes, of course, are not our friends nor our enemies. They are just snakes. Sometimes their actions help people, such as when they kill **rodents**, like mice and rats. Sometimes their actions are harmful, such as when a venomous snake bites a person. But snakes aren't trying to be helpful or harmful. They are just eating food and protecting themselves.

Snakes are an important part of the natural world. As **predators**, or hunters, they help control the numbers of smaller animals.

Snakes are normally shy and live secret lives. A snake's colors help it hide easily among leaves or rocks, on sand or branches. A snake doesn't want to be seen.

Often, we don't see snakes until we've nearly stepped or sat upon them! When we're that close, we may frighten the snake. A frightened snake usually hurries away, but it may bite.

Sea snakes are highly venomous, but like most snakes, they have no reason to bite when left alone. The diver is curious, not frightened.

DANGEROUS SNAKES

Most snakes are not venomous. But even if a **nonvenomous** snake bites, the wound should be cleaned carefully. Bites of venomous snakes are dangerous. Bites of North American venomous snakes seldom cause anyone's death, however. That is because people can usually reach a doctor quickly.

Any bite of a venomous snake can cause great pain. And the bite could cause permanent injury or even death. A person who has been bitten by a venomous snake should always seek out a doctor.

Basically timid, snakes like to lie quietly hidden in their surroundings. This is a sidewinder, a type of rattlesnake of the American Southwest.

Most human deaths from snake bite happen in the **rural** areas of Africa and Asia. A person there may face many problems in trying to reach a doctor. The snakes in these regions are also highly venomous.

Would a venomous snake's bite kill you if you did not get medical help? This would depend upon several things, such as the kind of snake. It would depend partly upon how much venom the snake forced into you. Your size, age, and overall health would also be important factors.

Nonvenomous snakes like the smooth green snake are harmless to people. The green snakes eat insects and spiders. Rough green snakes are climbers.

ANTIVENIN

The best treatment for a snake bite is **antivenin**. Antivenin is a medicine in liquid form. A doctor injects it with a needle.

Antivenin is made from snake venom and the blood of living horses. (The horses are not hurt by the process of making antivenin.)

In the United States, one type of antivenin works against the bites of copperheads, cottonmouths, and rattlesnakes. Coral snake bites are treated with another type of antivenin.

The colorful San Francisco garter snake is an endangered species because of habitat loss.

The tree-loving Jamaican boa, found nowhere except on the island of Jamaica, is perhaps the most endangered snake in North America.

The green mamba of Africa, like many venomous snakes, is as dangerous as it is beautiful.

MYTHS

For thousands of years, snakes have been part of tall tales and **myths**. People falsely believed, for example, that milk snakes drank directly from cows. Some people still mistakenly believe that snakes are slimy to the touch.

A myth in the Far East states that the mark on a cobra's hood is Buddha's fingerprint.

Some people say that you can tell a rattlesnake's age by the number of rattles on its tail. That, too, is a myth.

North America's copperheads, cottonmouths, and rattlesnakes are closely related. One type of antivenin treats bites from all three, including the cottonmouth here.

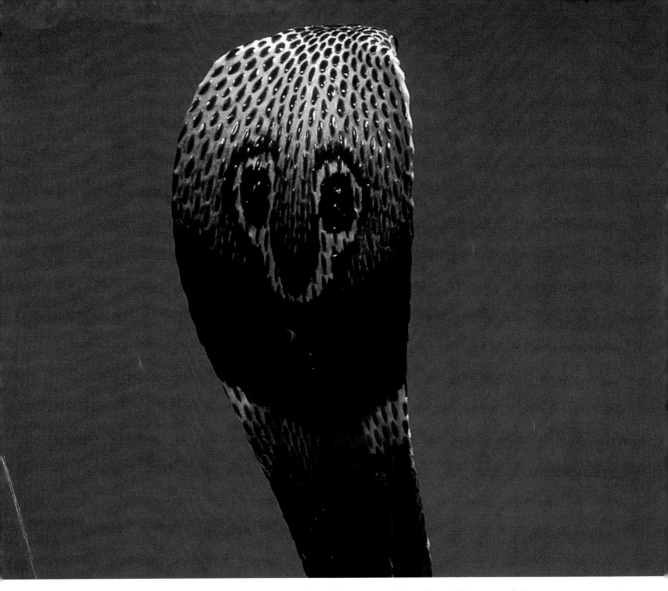

Old stories from the Far East say that Buddha put his fingerprint on the back of the cobra's hood.

18

USING SNAKES

Many people value snakes as pets. Most captive snakes become quite relaxed with their owners. Nonvenomous snakes usually can be handled safely. Only professionals should try to keep and handle venomous snakes.

No one should keep a snake of any kind, however, without knowing how to care for it. Snake ownership is best left to zoos and **serpentariums.** Serpentariums show large numbers of captive snakes.

In addition to being valued as pets, some snakes are wanted for their skin. Snakeskin is used to make leather goods, such as boots.

SAVING SNAKES

Being killed for their skins is not the biggest problem snakes face. The biggest problem is loss of **habitat**.

Habitat is the place where an animal lives. It could be a desert, forest, grassland, or some other place.

Many kinds of snakes are at risk of becoming **extinct**. This is largely because their living space has been destroyed.

Rattlesnake roundups in the western United States destroy thousands of rattlesnakes each year. As rattler numbers drop, rodent and rabbit numbers climb. Snakes receive little protection, even in the USA.

Some states have begun to protect certain snakes, like the eastern indigo and timber rattlesnake. But no snake can survive without a place to live. People can help save snakes by saving their habitat.

GLOSSARY

antivenin (AN ti ven in) – drug made from snake venom and horse blood to fight the effects of a venomous snake's bite

extinct (ik STINGKT) – no longer existing

habitat (HAB eh tat) – the special kind of place in which an animal lives, such as the desert

myth (MITH) – an often repeated story or tale which is not true, but is often believed

nonvenomous (NAHN ven uh mus) – refers to a snake that does not produce venom, a poison

predators (PRED uh terz) – animals that hunt and kill other animals for food

rodent (ROW dent) – any one of several mammals, such as rats, mice, and squirrels, that have teeth designed for gnawing

rural (RER ul) – an outlying area, away from any city

serpentarium (ser pen TAYR ee um) – a place which houses and shows snakes (serpents)

venomous (VEN uh mus) – refers to a snake that produces venom, a poison

FURTHER READING

Find out more about snakes with these helpful books:

Greer, Dr. Allen. **Reptiles**, Time Life, 1996
McCarthy, Colin. **Reptile**. Alfred Knopf, 1991
Schnieper, Claudia. **Snakes, Silent Hunters**. Carolrhoda, 1995
Simon, Seymor. **Snakes**. Harper Collins, 1994

INDEX